The Haunting Presences

of the

Omni Bedford Springs

John Sabol

~ *John G. Sabol* ~

Also by John Sabol...

Ghost Excavator (2007)
Ghost Culture (2007)
Gettysburg Unearthed (2007)
Battlefield Hauntscape (2008)
The Anthracite Coal Region (2008)
The Politics of Presence (2008)
Bodies of Substance, Fragments of Memory (2009)
Phantom Gettysburg (2009)
Digging Deep (2009)
The Re-Haunting(s) of Gettysburg (2010)
The Haunted Theatre (2011)
Ghost Culture Too (2012)
Beyond the Paranormal (2012)
Digging-Up Ghosts (2nd publishing, 2013)
Burnside Bridge (2013)
The Gettysburg Experience (2013)
The Absence Above, A Presence Below (2013)
The Production of Haunted Space (2013)
Centralia, Pennsylvania (2013)
The Ghost Excavation (2013)
The Good Death and the Civil War (2014)
Centralia: A Vision of Ruin (2014)
Altered States: Making the Extraordinary
Ordinary Again (2014)
Archaeology and Ghost Research: A Relational Entanglement (2014)
Performances in Haunted Space: An Afterlife in Ruin (2014)
Haunting Presences, Ruins, and Ghostly Entanglements (2015)
The Afterlife of Centralia: Presences in a Landscape of
Destruction (2015)
An Archaeology Without Borders: Performance Excavations in
Embedded/Entangled Fields (2016)
Ghost Hunt: Exploding the Myths/Exploring the Possibility (2016)
The Haunting of the Omni Bedford Springs Resort and Spa (2016)

The Haunting Presences

of the

Omni Bedford Springs

Ghost Excavator Books, Inc. TM©

Bedford, Pennsylvania, USA

ISBN-13: 978-1544847313
ISBN-10: 1544847319

Ghost Excavation Books, Inc.™©
A division of C.A.S.P.E.R. Research Center™©,
Bedford, PA, USA
www.ghostexcavation.com

Preface

"But when from a long-distant past nothing subsists, after the people are dead, after the things are broken and scattered, still, alone, more fragile but with more vitality, more unsubstantial, more persistent, more faithful, the smell and taste of things remain poised a long time, like souls, ready to remind us, waiting and hoping for their moment, amid the ruins of all the rest; and bear unfaltering, in the tiny and almost impalpable drop of their essence, the vast structure of recollection".

- *Marcel Proust*

Modernity's break with tradition, and its loss of the capacity for 'spontaneous' remembering due to the continued saturation of new experiences and technologies, is not in evidence at Bedford Springs. The presence of the past there is counter to what Nora (1989:7) said when he wrote that "we speak so much of memory because there is so little of it left".

At Bedford Springs, seeped in and surrounded by re-collected things, beings, and atmospheres, remembrance comes in multiple forms: historical documents and photographs, in the exhibition and use of antique furniture, in the daily practices of a contemporary, modern resort. It even comes in the form of 'ghost tours' that emphasize the archaeological and anthropological routes and roots of layers of embedded memories. Finally, it materializes as 'ghostly presences' who remain attached to that unique and lasting Bedford Springs experience.

<u>Photo 1</u>: An Object of Historical Memory

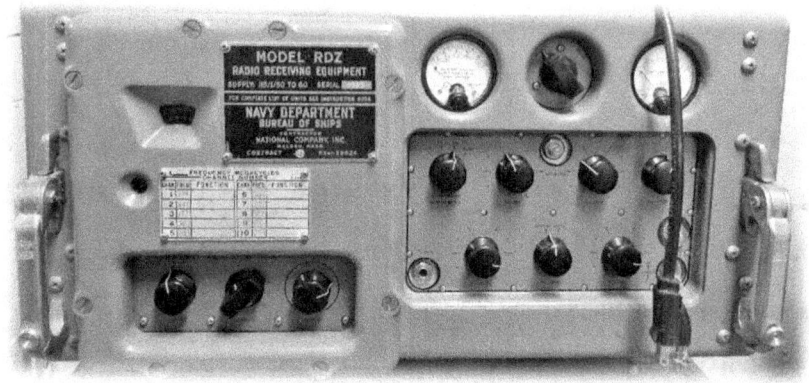

If memory is a performance of the past in the present, it is vital that we take into account the material world (the objects of remembrance), the space in which these objects are located, and the medium through which performances of memory (as movements of beings, both present and past) takes place. The past that is remembered goes beyond common understandings of people, objects, and spaces, or in the deliberate commemorations, such as the historical displays. The 'ghost tour' explores how 'other' presences remember their memories of the "Bedford Springs Experience".

Bedford Springs, a setting that generates multiple layers of memories, constructs meaning from these experiences, not as a 'scripted' text but in acts of behavior. Through social practices, guests both 'haunt' there (by returning) and cause 'ghosts' to materialize by repeating past social acts that continue there. Thus, both the 'atmosphere' of the resort itself, and the cultural responses of contemporary guests, create a social ambiance of continuing haunting presence.

The contemporary guest, as tourist, becomes part of the 'ghost story' of Bedford Springs, as they experience its hospitality and engage in activities there. But the full impact of the ghost stories becomes meaningful when it is actualized in a haunting experience that replicates past acts of behavior.

This haunting experience is more than a symbolic (or metaphoric) quality of action with the 'ghosts of place'. It also involves the materiality of past things in contemporary spaces of the resort complex. The guests as presences who become embedded in their daily activities entangle with social relations and material settings that involve past and present.

The 'ghostly' traces left behind (memories that materialize) and historical documents and objects create haunting accounts of what happened (and is happening) there. The ghost tours links these traces of materializing memories and historical displays of documents and objects. This creates an entanglement between what guests did in the past and what relationships can become manifest when similar acts to the past are enacted today.

The historical setting, the historical display of documents and objects, and the ghost tour narrative serve as 'background cues' to what becomes the 'haunting' nature of Bedford Springs. They tie together the ephemeral and the enduring.

<u>Photos 2/3</u>: Space of Remembrance in Layers of Memory (Reynolds Room- 1955; Duke of Bedford Library- 2017)

Photo 2:

Photo 3:

Introduction

Are uncanny materializations a form of mundane tasks (as opposed to a dramatic or horrific event) that reiterate a presence of the past that may occur on numerous occasions in particular spaces? Over time, do these mundane tasks involve the gradual formation of patterns of habit and repetition (a 'habit memory') that become a 'taskscape' in particular places? Does this 'taskscape' come to be popularly called by some a 'haunting'? Do they embody and express collective social values, proper etiquette, and cultural customs and norms (even pragmatic concerns)?

Is such a 'haunted taskscape' a part of the "Bedford Springs Experience", its tradition as a place where "best friends forever" first met? Do some former guests there remain (as a 'guestscape'), perhaps because they are still searching for that 'lost', but not forgotten 'best friend'? Or, are some attached to some unique experience (as former guest) or task (as former staff) they may have had there? This attachment to a situation, task, or event (as experienced) in a particular space at a specific place, results, in some instances, to a love of place: "the human beings affective ties with the material environment" (Yi-Fu Tuan 1974:93).

This can result in a place becoming the "carrier of emotionally-charged events or perceived as a symbol" (Ibid: 93). These are circumstances that do not need to involve tragedy, suffering, death, or unsolved mysteries, such as those that are popularly perceived to be causes of a haunting in ghost hunting lore.

In tourism, the past is regarded as an important tool "to sell the present more effectively in a process where the interest of different stakeholders appear to converge: history helps to culturalize consumption by bridging the gap between past and present….culture and leisure…" (Melotti 2016:132).

The consumer of recreation and places of leisure (such as Bedford Springs) are usually defined by their relation to place. In a hypermodern context, that relation and flow of movement can be perceived as the guest choosing a comforting (relaxing) or compliant (recreational) image. Following such trends, which tend to privilege what is represented at the location, the guest follows a pacified retreat into that world of comfortable surroundings. The result is a normative spacing of things, activities, and people. History there, revealed principally in displays of historical documents and historical photographs of past guests, complements this comforting and compliant image.

Many guests, including those at Bedford Springs, however, become mesmerized by the 'trick' of the seen. This can obliterate the usually unsensed and 'unscened'. The question then becomes this: what usually unseened and ignored sense of presence ought one might include as a tourist experience? What other sense of place can be felt in the Bedford Springs experience?

All landscapes, especially those adapted to tourism and recreation (like Bedford Springs), are continually in motion. But underneath, or hidden (at most times) from these surface flows are these other unseen and unsensed performances, as a continuing process of a particular 'other' presence of the past that remains.

<u>Photo 4</u>: History and the Making of 'Presence' at Bedford Springs

Photo 5: 'Making' of 'Presence'

In a previous book, (Sabol 2016), I outlined a number of ghost stories that are associated with Bedford Springs, those that are usually unseen and unsensed by most contemporary guests. The 'guestscapes' and 'taskscapes' that haunt Bedford Springs are continually re-made. They add an attracting (and affecting) ambiance to the contemporary 'Bedford Springs Experience'. Are the hauntings there another form of (e)'scape', albeit a 'hauntscape'? Do they become accretional: do they gather together with contemporary acts and behaviors, becoming more layered with memories, spaces made more hauntingly complex?

We have seen (and experienced) this process of increasing haunting phenomenon taken during our 'ghost tours' there. Guests have reported uncanny experiences during the tour, and some report haunting manifestations afterwards, during their remaining stay at the hotel. Has the entanglement of a specific tour that relates to stories that deal with the hauntings of Bedford Springs provided the contemporary guests who participate in the tour with a unique emotional experience of their own?

Does this uncanny, 'other' emotional experience translate into a real sense of 'ghostly presence' at Bedford Springs? Does it create a certain "emotional habitus" (Illouz 2007) between embedded past presences and the contemporary guest? Is a cultural resonance established between the contemporary guest and embedded past presences through the enactment of (or telling of) past social practices performed at Bedford Springs, while participating on the ghost tour?

Context-specific manifestations, those related to the tour, are, I propose, a direct effect of our storytelling on the tour, in combination with the guests re-iterating many of the same activities (during and afterwards) of those told in the ghost stories. Are 'ghostly presences' listening and responding to the cadences, rhythms, narratives, and flow of the tour? Does this result in a number of potential 'future effects' that affect the perception of contemporary reality of today's guests at Bedford Springs?

Do those past presences who may become attached to particular memories of the 'Bedford Springs experience' an example of "extended emotions" (Krueger and Szanto 2016)? Is this 'attachment effect' heightened by features of material culture at Bedford Springs, such as the historical displays and furniture? Do these mediums of presentation (extended emotions and material culture) extend the 'message' of a 'haunting' presence at Bedford Springs? Does it result in the manifestation of an extended emotional consciousness that continues to interact within its memories in various contemporary spaces of Bedford Springs?

This entangled process of extended emotions, material culture, and social interaction on the ghost tour may be "partially off-loaded onto the environment in that they loop through our ongoing interactions with different parts of our material culture" (Ibid: 9), such as the historical documents and photographs, perhaps even the 'etched' window panes in the Duke of Bedford Library room? Does it extend this affective 'haunting atmosphere' at Bedford Springs?

Does attending the ghost tour set the 'stage' for a real, not merely theatrical, change in the Bedford Springs social reality? Does it modify how guests "perceive….the event, in part because others' reactive behavior and emotional responses may become constituents of MY experience" (Ibid: 13)? Does it become real? Read on….or better still, come to Bedford Springs, if you are in the area, and join us on the tour!

<u>Photo 6</u>: The Ghost Tour

Table of Contents

<u>Photos 7/8</u>: Doing Research in the 'Basement Museum'

Photo 7:

Photo 8:

Photographs

<u>The Presence of Past Presence(s)</u>

Guests at tourist locations, as a crucial part of the complex of leisure in the 21st century, rely on the 'stage authenticity' of the past, a representation of reality through a fabrication of real experience (cf. MacConnell 1973). Past presence is 'staged' through various guises, including re-enactments and history tours, historical displays, and historical photographs and objects (including period piece furniture).

In tourist destinations, the past is regarded as an important tool "to sell the present more effectively in a process where the interest of different stakeholders appear to converge: history helps to culturalize consumption by bridging the gap between past and present....culture and leisure...." (Melotti 2016:132). At Bedford Springs, the past and present mingle together in various ways.

<u>Photo 9</u>: Historical Displays: Bedford Springs

Photo 10: Historical Display at Bedford Springs:

An Alcove of Historical Postcards

Photo 11: Historical Photographs in the Crystal Dining Room

Examples of 'staged authenticity' are well-represented at Bedford Springs. But there is more. The 'ghost tour' is meant to occupy that space within this 'staged authenticity' than can provide the possibility of a real, albeit uncanny, experience of the Bedford Springs past. The spaces where ghosts are held to occupy are constructed as being authentic, through the very experience of ghostly presences.

To get this sense of a Bedford Springs 'past' experience, as both an historical landscape as well as a counter-historical 'haunted' one (where the sense of time 'stands still'), we must alter our perception and meaning of landscape and physical environment. The Oxford Dictionary defines landscape as foremost a 'view', a scenery, the "object of one's gaze". Bedford Springs certainly has beautiful views to behold. Its setting is majestically-placed and historic, making it a frequent object of return of many past and present guest's gaze.

But it is also something more. From a phenomenological perspective, it can be perceived as "embodied sets of relationships between places, a structure of human feeling, emotion…movement and practical activity…" (Tilley 2004:25). From this perspective, a sense of Bedford Springs is understood radically different from a simple gaze. It becomes a dynamic process of entanglement between guest and space in "a consideration of fluidity, transition, and motion" (Benediktson & Lund 2010:3).

One way in which this can be understood is through a dynamic relation between the contemporary guest and their past counterpart, the 'ghosts' that still remain attached to their memories of Bedford Springs. This changes the concept of Bedford Springs space from something gazed upon to something sensed of that Bedford Springs past. Bedford Springs has much to sense. This sense of presence goes beyond its original limestone foundation (which can still be seen in certain areas of the resort complex). It's more than its architectural features, its additions and renovations, the facilities and services that complement the landscape space.

Photos 12/13: The Bedford Springs Historical Landscape

Photo 12:

Photo 13:

<u>Photo 14</u>: The Contemporary Landscape

But is this 'past present', represented in the form of 'ghostly presences', there merely a consequence of Bedford Springs having a long and varied emotional (and entertaining) history? Have perceived haunted locations, like Bedford Springs, become a technological unconsciousness, a 'playground' for 'ghost hunting', one in which content (and meaning) has evolved into the "bending of bodies-with-environments to a specific set of addresses without the benefit of any cognitive inputs" (Thrift 2008:91)?

The technological unconscious that has popularly become 'ghost hunting' and 'paranormal investigation' is "a prepersonal substrate of guaranteed correlations, assured encounters, and therefore unconsidered anticipations" (Ibid: 91). It has changed the 'face' of the 'ghost' as an encounter with a technological measurement, not a 'ghost story'. No longer is 'ghostly presence' a 'dead human'. It is a recorded 'anomaly', or a deviation in the physical environment, an energy field that envelopes particular spaces. This contemporary 'para-movement', largely inspired by TV programming and filmic renditions of 'hauntings', has changed the 'idea' of 'ghostly presence'. It brings into being a new variety of aestheticism of detection that locates and produces a desired effect and affect that becomes the present state of a 'haunting' and its 'ghosts'.

The 'idea' of a 'ghost' as 'verbal formula' – or the name that is attached to a 'haunting'-may remain unchanged. They still call a 'ghost' a 'ghost'. But "if the problem to which it is addressed is altered, then so is the idea" (Condren 1985:111). If a 'haunting' is 'addressed' by ghost tech devices, instead of being a past cultural, conscious being, then the 'ghost' becomes an 'anomaly', albeit a 'paranormal' one. It becomes a measurement of environmental deviation. This 'anomalous' designation maintains ghost hunting's fringe status as something still beyond explanation.

As John Potts (2006) suggests, "the contemporary ghost – as charted, recorded, depicted, analyzed, classified, and explained on the web…perform the work of fusing magic and technology…They are hybrid ghosts, in an age that wants to believe in the powers of science but is drawn with an equal force by the lure of the unknown" (2006:90).

Is the perceived presence of 'ghosts' at Bedford Springs a conformity to this contemporary 'idea' of a technological-unconscious concept of forms of anomalous energy materializations? Has the perception of these technologically-framed 'ghosts' become a part of the experience of 'energetic' emotion that merely serves to entertain the contemporary guest? Is it because the place displays the presence of the past in multiple ways? I don't think so…..

Bedford Springs is a place of action, a landscape of complex temporalities, as well as one of relaxation and recreation. Social behaviors there provide the foundation for activity. Many of these social activities reiterate those of the resort's history. The palimpsest of architectural features, some of which date back to the early 19th century (like the Stone Inn and the kitchen/Defibaugh

Table area), provide the contemporary guest (and the 'attached' ghost) with both possibilities and constraints for future conduct and manifesting presence.

At Bedford Springs, the symbols and objects of different ages are brought together, making it truly a 'timely' place to experience multiple pasts. It is a place where life was (is) lived with an awareness of many different past presences, including the 'ghostly' ones. It is a place where many of those pasts literally reach out and touch the present. It is a place where these links and connections amount to more than the sum of observable (visible) components.

The images, <u>and</u> a sense of the past, create a distinctive approach one receives of time there. It is not a passage toward something. It is rather a series of interconnecting stories that link past and present. At Bedford Springs, the culture of different periods comes together in a single design.

On one level, or strata of memory, the resort demonstrates how the past can be recreated and reused with still present meaning. On another, 'ghostly presences' stand-in for a different characteristic of the presence of the past. Together, they form a unique blending (past and present) of an entanglement between experience, memory, remembrance, resonance, and re-iteration of practices. Both prevent the present guest from forgetting what happened in history at Bedford Springs, and 'what' ('who') still remains there.

What the hauntings at Bedford Springs show is that two temporal 'scapes' exist simultaneously at Bedford Springs. One is a 'hauntscape' that continues, consisting of 'attached' entities who 'perform' routine, habitual acts in context-specific spaces whose actions are a part of their memories of their stay at Bedford Springs. Some of these are residual recordings, non-interactive manifestations that replay without conscious effort. The perception of women dressed in Victorian-era clothing, reported throughout the hotel, is an example of this. The sounds of 'Big Band Music' playing in the Eisenhower Ballroom is another example. A Morse code transmission we recorded near the Reagan Ballroom, in the hallway leading toward the restaurant complex, is still another. The other is an interactive presence whose conscious acts are sensed and reported by both guests and staff. The little girl in Victorian dress who haunts the indoor pool area is an example of this interactive presence.

The other 'scape' is the resort's contemporary 'taskscape', the array of staff who serve the guests today. They 'perform' to a different audience, but do not go unobserved by those who remain behind from the past. This is verified by the frequent, and unexpected, encounters between staff and 'ghostly presences'. Thus, today at Bedford Springs two temporally-distinct, coincident and inter-penetrating, 'scapes' can (and do) occupy the same space there.

These two 'scapes' represent two different perceptions of time at Bedford Springs:

- There is individual 'haunting time'. This is the habitual and social acts of former guests moving through the resort complex. These movements are based, I propose, on memories of particular acts in specific spaces of the resort complex; and

- There is 'public time', the flow and movement of contemporary guests and staff through the resort complex.

This heterogeneous time creates an entangled space-time continuum. There is a sense of living in history, with displayed historical documents, historical photos and furniture, and 'ghostly presences'. There is also a sense of 'living the moment', the daily routines, social interactions, and extra events of a contemporary resort complex. These temporalities are not only diverse, they are also dependent on one another. Social practices go on or through time and space, yet constitute different 'timings' of action in space-time. The stories that are told on the ghost tour (see below for more information about these tours) emphasize this uncanny overlapping of temporalities in the public spaces of the resort complex.

Social interaction between the two 'times' occur frequently, irregardless of the 'time' of day. There is no specific 'dead time', except on TV and in fictionalized accounts of hauntings. There is continuous ruptures in temporality. It is when the past returns to alter the passage of time. It is when 'ghosts' appear and are sensed. This is not a philosophical issue (a question of belief) or a religious one (a questioning of faith). It is what people, both guest and staff, do experience there. This entanglement between time, space, memory, movement, and social/habitual acts creates a series of "time-space routines" and a Bedford Springs "place-ballet" (cf. Seamon 1980).

Bedford Springs does not exist as a stable space over which clock or calendrical time pass. It can become a different place at any time (through the manifestation of residual presences), or during specific times (as when contemporary behaviors resonate with those of the past resulting in the manifestation of an interactive presence). Time is better understood as a space-time that is defined by social interaction. Thus, we can think of Bedford Springs, not as a simple and single landscape, but rather as several distinct, yet relationally-overlapping space-times (cf. Dawdy 2016).

These space-time ruptures are plurimedial: they come from multiple different sources, which now include incidents of perceived presence that are occurring during the ghost tours (see below). Such different references result in various versions of both haunting phenomenon, and, in the case of a visual experience, different individual presences (perhaps from different time periods). Such plurimediality prompts a deeper level of engagement with the Bedford Springs experience. It also changes the experience a person has from a ghost story (told on a tour, or read about on social media or in a book) to my ghost story.

The result of these temporal displacements is that what matters, at any given time, might be "out of time". This 'out of time' might manifest as the presence of someone (perhaps dressed differently), the movement of something (from one place to another in a room), or something becoming temporally missing (such as wrist watches in the indoor pool area).

Do these displacements really matter? Do they create a different Bedford Springs experience, one that adds, rather than being a concern, to the guest's stay there? The ghost tour focuses on the positive side of these 'ghostly presences': former guests who remain attached to the memories of their experiences there. It is to the nature of the ghost tour that I now turn.

<u>Photo 15</u>: Did this Social Interaction Create a Future 'Ghostly Presence'?

<u>Photo 16</u>: Did this Past Presence Create a Contemporary 'Haunting Presence'?

July 1896 –

The Ghost Tour

Photo 17: A Recent Bedford Springs Ghost Tour

In the normal and daily reality of living, people are caught-up in situations, events, and things which are a natural attitude toward life, including relaxation and recreation. At Bedford Springs, the ghost tour is an attempt to focus on other questions and interests: what experiential meaning does a place like Bedford Springs have for guests, a meaning that goes beyond this 'natural' attitude toward relaxation and recreation.

How do different contemporary guests experience this 'other' life there, one that pays homage to the Bedford Springs past? On the ghost tour, we consider these lived experiences as historical 'afterlives', which others consider 'dead and buried'. We focus on those Bedford Springs stories which still can be sensed and experienced.

On the ghost tour, we repeat and mimic those past activities in the very spaces where they originally occurred, even though the contemporary space may have changed. An example of this would be the contemporary Duke of Bedford Library. At other times, this space served as 'Reynold's Bar', a music room, and a space where billiards was played. Thus, the space has multiple layers of different memories attached to it. We use these different layers of memory to create social context-specific scenarios that are directly related to these memories.

As we move across these spaces of the resort on the tour, contemporary participants on the tour may sense individual entities 'detach' themselves from the background, and become interested in the flow of movement and what is being said in the stories we tell the guests. Some may reveal themselves in various ways (such as sounds, smells, touch, and even visually).

In this way, the contemporary guest on the ghost tour gains a richer familiarity with the historical and affecting nature of their surroundings as a kind of 'sensory narrative' of past presence. This intersects with the temporal narrative, spanning decades, of the historical displays, photographs, and other visuals that are dispersed throughout the hotel. Furthermore, have some of the documents and photographs "abducted" (Gell 1998) qualities of their time? Are they still residually-charged, something more than just 'dead matter'? Do they contribute to the 'haunting' nature of Bedford Springs?

These 'things left behind' result in a "percolation of time" (Witmore 2009), becoming a living (and 'haunting') presence of the past in the present. Such displays provide new possibilities for perceiving, thinking, and acting which the ghost tour reinforces through the stories that are told to the guests.

These stories – alternative experiences – are those that guests there rarely seek, or even think about. They differ from 'traditional' history in that some of the historical 'dead and buried' are not 'dead and buried'! These 'ghostly presences' are a form of 'ruin memory': what remains of the past in fragmented form, or as traces of past human consciousness. It is in those situations, movements, and people who are not remembered (because time, context, and people have passed), acknowledged (by the present), or awaiting interpretation (because the experience is still perceived as an 'anomaly'), that we retrieve and give contemporary meaning to on our ghost tour.

The result is a bond or continuity that occurs between people and history. What this means is that people are not affectively confined to a particular point of time-space, but become distributed beings: the continuation of presence, as something of their being, experience, intention, personality, and memory continue through time. Does this also include, in some instances, a part of past conscious behavior, one based on the memory of experiences one had at Bedford Springs?

This possibility can lead one to recognize previously unnoticed connections and relationships between objects, space, and phenomena. The historical artifacts become 'props' for a 'haunting stage' through which the ghost tour moves. It provides the participants and 'guests' ('ghostly presences'), as audience, with an "extension of perceiving" (Gibson 1986:258), one that still haunts the corridors, halls, and rooms of the resort complex..

By making these stories archaeologically useful, as a record of continuing presence within layers of memory in particular spaces of the resort complex, we bring them back to life, but not as an 'anomaly', something paranormal, or a measured environmental deviation. They become a continuing form of life, an 'afterlife' of the Bedford Springs historical experience.

Archaeologist James Deetz (1998) has pointed out that a good story is one that is remembered, has meaning, and can leave listeners with new questions to think about. Some of the tour guests not only remember the ghost stories, they have experiences relating to these stories. The linking of a story to a personal experience lays a groundwork for guests to form a relationship with both 'ghostly presence' and Bedford Springs.

This relationship is more than experiencing the "ghosts of place" outlined by Michael Bell, an environmental sociologist. Bell's (1997) "ghosts of place" are simply the human ability to sense the presence of an absent past:

"Who has not had that sense while creeping into some room....that someone unseen was watching" (1997:813).

The "ghosts of place" are a means, metaphorically speaking, to anchor past memories at historic places. At Bedford Springs, the situation is different. At Bedford Springs, though this anchor is made manifest through displays of historical documents and photographs, the 'ghostly presences' that are experienced there are context-specific manifestations that are relative to particular situations, events, sometimes even individuals that have occurred or visited there (like several who have experienced the 'ghost' of Daniel Webster). These 'ghosts of place' are not products of imagination and social construction (Bell 1997:831).

Photo 18: A 'Ghost' Photographed in the Pool Area (January 2017) (Photography Courtesy of Mike Stevenson)

<u>**Note**</u>**: This 'presence' was NOT visually seen at the time the photograph was taken. He only appears in the photograph.**

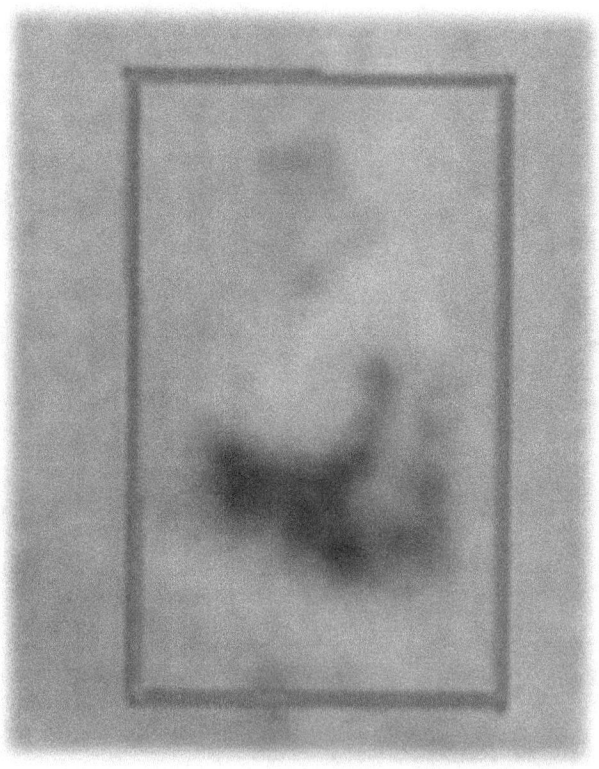

The Bedford Springs 'ghosts' are not mere 'ghosts'. They are historical entities, some even know personages. The 'ghost' at Bedford Springs is also not a representation of the past. The 'ghost' remains as a form of 'past life' that is still actively engaged in the memory of his/her 'Bedford Springs experience'. The 'ghosts' there become another authenticity of the power of attraction that is the 'Bedford Springs experience. Their manifestations do not 'ruin' that experience. They highlight it! They do this by complementing, in a parallel way, the normative spacing of things, practices, and guests at the resort.

At Bedford Springs, the presence of 'ghosts' is not focused on entertainment. During the tour, we take extreme care with the stories that we tell the guests. This means that we interpret the traces of manifesting presence and movement with sensitivity, resisting the temptation to 'invent' phantoms or exaggerate their appearances. This would only obscure and detract from their social and historical context.

We do not consider the appearance of 'orbs' as indicators of a haunting; nor do we talk about 'anomalies'. We also don't introduce any 'evidence' from 'ghost hunts' at Bedford Springs, and the 'meanings' that are implied from measurements and 'reactions' recorded on 'ghost tech' equipment, and reported by paranormal investigators.

The ghost tour, revealed through performance and storytelling, is the use of the archaeological imagination (together with data derived from the historical record). This archaeological imagination involves:

"A pervasive set of attitudes towards traces...the persistence of the past, the articulation of remains of the past with the present, recollecting, as a memory practice, bringing what is left of the past before the present..." (Shanks and Svabo 2013:91).

The tours emphasize the idea of historical and cultural context—specific 'ghosts'. This involves historical discontinuity (as 'ghostly'-embedded/attached presence) and cultural difference (relative to a particular society and socio-cultural etiquette and moral code). The majority of 'ghostly presences' that have been perceived there are from the Victorian Period (1835-1901), representing a large historical rupture.

The idea of the 'Victorian ghost' at Bedford Springs is a notion of a "time-located stage in a developmental process" (Mink 1987: 212). It is a 'time' in history that becomes embedded/attached. It does not end, but continues. This is important because the cultural difference between the Victorian guest and the contemporary one provokes diversity in the expression of specific 'ideas' regarding manifesting phenomenon: manifestations that occur will reflect Victorian-era characteristics.

Materializations do not occur without the proper input of patterns of Victorian etiquette, ones based on the moral codes of that period. Manifestations do not occur by simply asking questions and expecting answers on particular ghost tech devices, as a specific experience unfamiliar to Victorian society (though it was an era of great technological development).

Materializations are context-specific to Victorian Era social etiquette (dress code, lack of direct communication with females) and technological knowledge and experience in the use of devices (importance of photography; use of Morse code), or lack thereof (curiosity about wrist watches, for example). On the ghost tour, we perform and re-create not merely the ghost story, but a context-specific 'storyscape' in which guests can actively participate in the story of past lives.

This 'storyscape' of narration and participation creates a widening (though not beyond 'normal' = 'paranormal') sense of presence within the flow of contemporary resort reality. The stories are combined with real social means of how one might encounter these 'ghostly presences'. The potential encounter, unlike 'ghost hunting' or 'paranormal investigation', is socially, not technologically-based (the use of 'ghost detecting devices' and apps). Instead, they are based on 'acting' just like those guests of long ago, performing similar (and resonating) relaxational, recreational, and entertainment-based behaviors, some in combination with simple devices (both physical and social) historically used at Bedford Springs (such as photography, audio, and social conversation as participant-observation).

Photography has always been important at Bedford Springs. It allows for the development of a particular sensitivity – a dynamic connection between past and present, of place, event, and people. We have had several participants on the tour relate to us afterwards that some of the photographs they had taken on the tour contain 'additional' entities and/or images.

<u>Photo 19</u>: The Entanglement of Place, Event, and People

<u>Photo 20</u>: Another Example of the Entanglement of Place, Event, and People

The photograph and ghostly presence are entangled together at Bedford Springs. Such entanglements are also linked to the connections between photography, death, ghosts, and hauntings in the ethnographic literature (cf. Smith and Vokes 2008). In some ethnographic contexts, photographs and ghosts are referred to in a single term (Crocker 1993).

Like ghostly presence, photographs can "stand in for" relationships that cannot or can no longer be continued directly. Do the photographs exhibited on the walls of the Crystal Dining Room signify the continuation of the popular Bedford Springs phrase as a place where "best friends forever" continue? Such photographs unsettle everyday distinctions between the presence and absence of social relationships. They also demonstrate "an ability to affect the social milieu in which they become meaningful" (Smith and Vokes 2008:284).

At Bedford Springs, does the cultural context of these photographs (in a context of social dining) allow for intense experiences of the dead "living on"? There have been various reports of uncanny sounds, associated with invisible presences that have been heard in this dining room. Is this the effect of the photographs on contemporary guests and staff, or their effect on attached ghostly presences?

The use of cameras by participating guests on the tour are an integral component of the ghost tour experience:

- This happened here (revealed in historical and contemporary photos);
- This could have happened here (the ghost stories);
- This might happen here (a manifestation during the tour); and
- This is how one might capture that actual 'haunting' moment (the taking of photos).

The importance of photographs is readily displayed, as photos of former guests (especially those taken during the period 1890-1905) are widely distributed throughout the hotel complex. The taking of photographs is a specific cultural aesthetic that has been reinforced through the last 100+ years of Bedford Springs' history.

Photography becomes a direct resonating link to the past, adhering to certain historical cultural norms. Photographs represent "indisputable evidence that the trip was made, that the program was carried out, that fun was had" (Sontag 1977:9). At Bedford Springs, they may even provide evidence of a ghostly identity.

In a series of photos, mostly exhibited in the Crystal Dining Room, there are photographs of a man (dressed differently in each photograph), taken in 1895, that closely resembles the photo of a man (who was not visibly seen at the time) taken in the pool area in January 2017. Is this the 'ghost' of the man whose photography hang today in the Crystal Dining Room?

<u>Photo 21</u>: The Original Photograph (Photo Courtesy of Mike Stevenson)

<u>Photo 22</u>: A Close-Up of the Original (Photo Courtesy of Mike Stevenson)

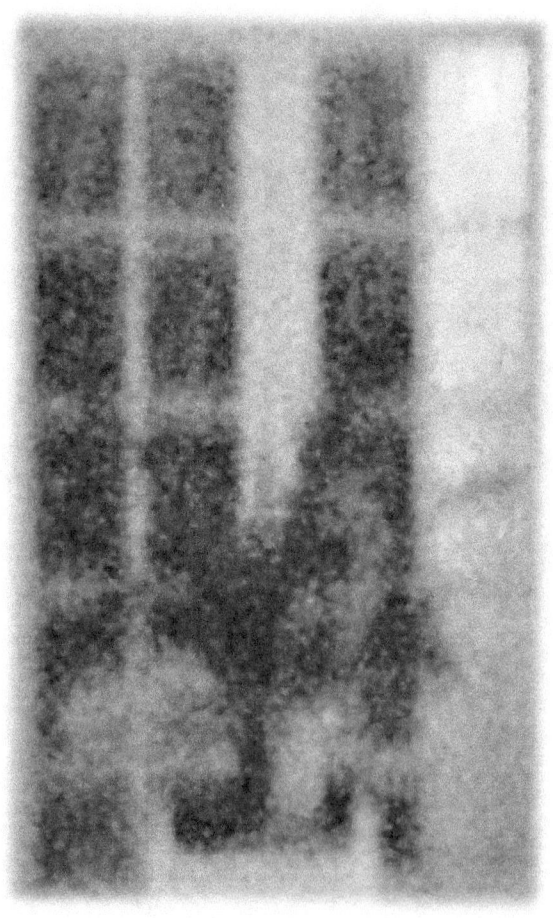

<u>Photos 23</u>: Photos Displayed in the Crystal Dining Room

Most ghost tours suggest and use 'ghost tech' interaction. At Bedford Springs, we suggest social interaction. These are behaviors in which both past and present guests find resonance, as many activities from the past continue today (such as relaxation, outdoor recreation, indoor swimming, eating and drinking, socializing, dances, etc.). But the participant must be cognizant of the social etiquette and moral codes of the particular period in which they attempt to immerse themselves.

The interactive nature of the ghost tour allows us to gather forensic data about the hauntings there. For us, this becomes a re-humanization of former perceived uncanny presences. It is putting people back into the past, not things or anomalies. As archaeologist Julian Thomas has said:

"We cannot put ourselves back into the heads of past people, but we must put people back into the spaces of the past" (1993:74).

This is a quest for understanding and interpretation, a meaning which does not involve environmental factors, the existence of non-human entities, or evil presences. This sensitivity to 'ghostly presence' changes the way one senses the surroundings. It does this by rendering some elements of the Bedford Springs resort environment and experience more real than others (cf. Schwartz 1985).

Holloway, in a recent study (2010), shows how material culture (such as historical documents and photographs) and social infrastructure (such as tours combined with stories of particular spaces) contribute to the experience of ghost tours. They enhance the sense that there might be something more to reality than the present worldview. This enhanced sense (affording the possibility of 'other' sensory and bodily experiences) contrasts with the carefully controlled and ordered modern resort environment. This is a 'cleaned-up' representation of the past that keeps that past at an 'arm's length' in displays and photos on walls.

During the ghost tour, we use a form of *deixis*. In Greek, 'deixis' means pointing something out.

During the ghost tour, we point to particular spaces in the hotel complex that link the world of the story to the real world of the Bedford Springs experience. Some of the tour participants extend the spatial distribution of the ghost stories by having a subsequent experience relative to the original story, in another part of the resort complex.

The guests on the tours have become active participants in the continuing histories of the ghost stories. Encounters with 'ghostly presences' have increased since the tours have begun. We can add numerous encounters to this 'other' Bedford Springs experience. Some of these are described below. Some would say that the tour influences the perception (as a form of suggestibility), increasing the guests expectations of a 'ghostly presence'. In this idea, it is the guest that is influenced by the tour.

I would look at it differently. I propose that it is the 'ghostly presences' who are inspired (affected) by the tour narrative and the guest interest in the stories and histories that are being told. These 'ghostly presences' differ from many 'ghost-hunting' modes of identifying phenomenon. They are not perceived (or sensed) as environmental anomalies or 'things', largely detected through electronic devices.

Their materialization and meaning becomes a creative process. It allows one to make context-specific entanglements in the process of perception, observation, experience, and social interaction. Contact becomes an interpretation through contingency. Contingency is to recognize multiple causes. Most ghost hunting does not acknowledge this. If something happens at a perceived haunted location, it is more than likely to be attributed to a 'ghostly presence', especially if it occurs on a 'ghost tech' device.

An interpretation of something as contingent "re-sorts sets of data which has been sorted out into separate categories by scientific method...it goes backwards through history to rediscover the kinds of connections made by people in their everyday life' (Muecke 2006:98). This is how we make connections between a sense, or perception of 'ghostly presence', and 'who' these ghosts may be and 'why' they manifest. It is based on past context-specific situations: a relationship between experience, emotion, and memory/remembrance.

The Bedford Springs 'ghosts' are cultural beings, not 'objects' and 'anomalies', who remain attached to particular memories of experiences that occurred at Bedford Springs. This is not the usual 'ghost hunting' meaning, derived from a perceived response to questions and/or demands to interact with a machine (usually unknown in the experience and memory of the 'ghost'). This questioning and those machines are not 'reliable witnesses'. Ghost tech has not "exorcised their ghosts so that they simplify and purify data, eliminating the unreliable and the contingent' (Ibid: 98).

There may be multiple sources that might cause the appearance of a haunting, none of which could relate to a past historical entity. But enacting stories, as context-specific situations that did occur in the past in specific spaces at Bedford Springs, and adding some sensory element (such as playing period music, taking photographs) can eliminate most of the contingencies that suggest other agencies involved in the manifestation.

If we eliminate the contingencies, then the entanglement between context-specific scenario and manifestation becomes a communicative cultural interaction. The entanglement of experience, memory, remembrance, space, time anchors the 'haunting' into a context-specific past behavior associated with a Bedford Springs past situation in one of the resort complex's spaces. The manifestation, if and when it occurs, does not remain an 'anomaly' or labeled a 'paranormal event'.

The immersive quality of the tour, as the experience of being part of something historical, provides guests with a sense of an embodied experience, especially when they have their own stories to add. Those individuals who follow our suggestions become active participants in a potential dramatic and emotional experience. By extension, those guests having their own experiences become part of the Bedford Springs story, albeit a ghost story. They are not merely a guest, but a part of its 'ghostly' presences.

What follows are new stories of 'haunting' experiences. These are ruptures, when the past enfolds into the present and a sense of past presence is felt. I hope that you are more than entertained by them. They are meant to show that the Bedford Springs Experience is not only about the present, but also about how the past is still with us. It is a past that is full of memories, yet memories that are still meaningful today.

The Haunting Continues...

Since the ghost tours began on a weekly basis in July 2016, reports of uncanny experiences, by both guests and staff, have increased. Whether this is the result of our ghost tours or the re-kindled interest in the history (albeit a haunted one) of Bedford Springs is not known. What follows are summaries of some of the personal stories of what guests on the tours have directly reported to us in person or via email.

These encounters are divided into three categories. This is based on the time the 'anomalous' event(s) occurred. No judgements are made here as to their authenticity. At present, they are considered subjective, personal experiences. They include the following:

- Pre-tour manifestations: these occurred before the tour and were reported to us during, or shortly after, the tour;

- Tour manifestations: these are simultaneous encounters with perceived 'ghostly presences' during the tour. Though subjectively perceived (usually by specific individuals not the whole tour group), they can serve as a baseline for further historical research and ethno-archaeological fieldwork; and

- Post-tour manifestations: these were reported to us via post-visit emails.

<u>Pre-Tour Manifestations</u>

Various guests have reported to us that they have sensed a child who moves in and around the indoor pool area. Some of these guests have related to us that the child's first name is "Anna", which corresponds to an "EVP" recorded in this area. The recording is said to be that of a child who gives her name as "Anna" or "Hannah" (Wilson 2013:58).

During one of our Saturday tours, a couple accompanied by their young son, heard the story we told about "Anna". Afterwards, the boy's father told us that the previous day, they were all in the indoor pool. The father noticed his son was talking to someone in the area next to the door where guests would enter the pool. Coming closer, he saw that there was no one there. He asked his son "who" he was just talking to. The son replied that he was talking to a little girl who was standing a few feet away, and didn't he see her. The father told us that he did not see the little girl.

Various female guests on the tour told us they have experienced a presence in the "Ladies Room" (days earlier), located outside the pool entrance (along the hallway leading toward the Spa section of the complex.

Photo 24: The Bathroom Area

Another female guest reported to us that she sensed a presence in the bathroom near the 1796 Restaurant. She reported that she heard the sounds of footsteps, but upon inspection no one was seen. In the same bathroom, there was also a report of one of the doors to a private stall was being pushed on, as if someone was attempting to enter. No one was seen.

Photo 25: Bathroom Entrance

Dining in the Crystal Room, prior to the tour, some of the guests report feeling uneasy with the photos of past guests (mostly Late Victorian) on the wall as they dined. In particular, a number of them have felt uneasy about one photograph, a man who appears in several photographic poses in different parts of the dining area (but with different clothing in each).

Prior to the tour one night in February 2017, we took a friend on a tour of Bedford Springs which included the indoor pool. He took a series of photographs. In one, see below, it shows what appears to be a man standing at the far end of the pool area, in front of the glass door. He has one foot on a planter, and is looking upwards toward the 2nd floor.

The photo of the man in the Crystal Dining Room appears similar in appearance to that man recently photographed in the pool area. We have since been shown similar photos of what appears to be this same man, all taken in the indoor pool area. One of the photographs was taken by a Bedford Springs staff member, and another by a guest while on the tour. The man appears in both these photographs behind (not in front of) the glass doors. He appears to be clothed similarly in all three contemporary photographs, which appears to be Late Victorian. This does not appear to be a 'residual' manifestation, as he is reacting to contemporary décor. The glass doors were not part of the original pool area, and the planter is relatively a new addition, and is not there all of the time in this same location.

The presence thus appears to be interacting with changes in the contemporary environment. "He" also changes his position in the various contemporary photographs. In two of them, he is behind the glass door. In the third, he appears in front of them. This movement suggests that this presence is "interactive".

Photo 26: The Indoor Pool Presence (Photo Courtesy of Mike Stevenson)

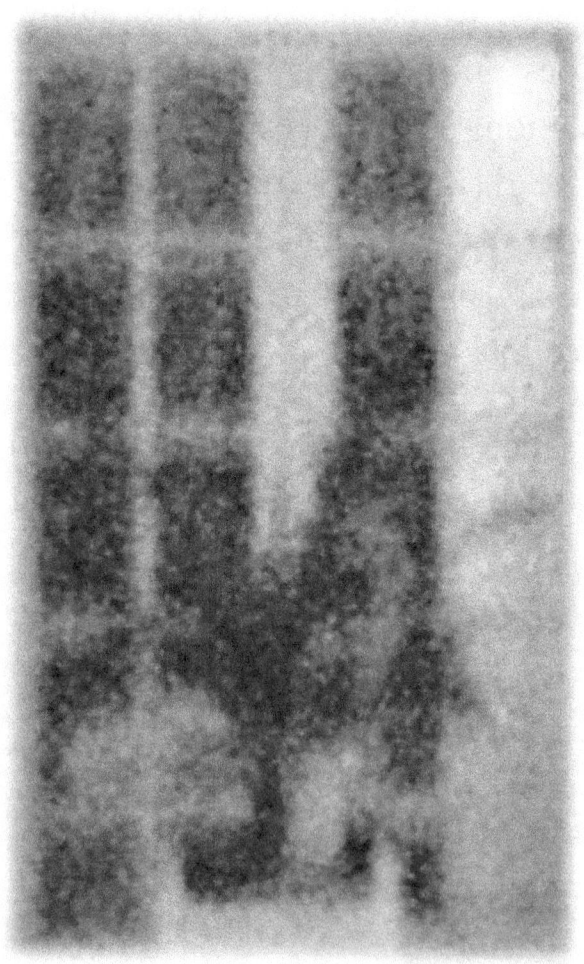

This same staff member also showed us another photo, taken at the same time as her previous one, of what appears to be a dark, solid 'shadow' figure on the 2nd floor of the indoor pool. In this same location in November, during a late night investigation, we saw a similar figure dart in and out of the columns there. When we approached the figure, it moved back into the darkness and disappeared.

Is the figure of the man below looking-up at this figure on the 2nd floor? Even though the photo (by Mike Stevenson) and the 'shadow' photo (by the staff member) were not taken at the same time, the gaze of the figure below is looking in the direction and location where the 'shadow' figure was photographed.

Various guests have reported to us of water in their rooms (in the sink and shower) turning on and off at various times throughout the night. These occurrences have been reported to appropriate staff, and may not be a paranormal event.

Tour Manifestations

During the ghost tour, we have had a number of participants report anomalous experiences. Guests continue to identify the name "Anna" as the presence of a little girl in the indoor pool area. We always, before entering this location, ask the guests to think of the name of this entity, or if they 'sense' a name, to tell us after we all enter the solarium in the pool area. We then write the name in front of them (but hidden from their view), and then ask them what name comes to mind.

Many of the guests who correctly identify the name of the little girl as "Anna" have subsequent uncanny experiences in their rooms (sounds, movement of personal items, etc.). No suggestion, however, of 'spirit attachment' is assumed at this time until a controlled investigation is undertaken.

One of our tour guests, who stated that she was a sensitive, reported to us, after the completion of the tour, that she 'saw' a little girl in the pool area. She said that the 'little girl' was listening to our stories we told in the solarium. We did not see her, nor did any of the other tour participants. We remain open, however, to this possibility based on the number of 'sightings' of the little girl by others (not connected to the tour).

During another tour, we had a dog accompany one of the guests. In the solarium, while talking about the appearances of the little girl, the dog suddenly appeared agitated, reacting to something in the solarium doorway when the name "Anna" was mentioned. As it focused its attention on the doorway, people turned to look but saw nothing there.

<u>Photo 27</u>: The Solarium Doorway

In the public Ladies Bathroom, located in the hallway leading toward the spa, there have been frequent reports by women (see above) of being touched on their lower legs. This only occurs to women who are wearing pants, not dresses. Is this the little girl, "Anna" from the indoor pool (located in close proximity to these bathrooms)? If she is from the Late Victorian Period (she is said to be dressed so), is she reacting to the wearing of pants by the women (certainly not a 'fashionable' way to dress in the Victorian Period)?

In the "Daniel Webster Room", adjacent to the "Crystal Dining Room", one of our tour participants reported that a man, sitting in one of the chairs there, was listening to our conversation. She 'identified' him as the same individual whose portrait hangs on the wall there, Daniel Webster. No one else on the tour saw the man sitting there. Also, in this room, a number of guests on the tour (both male and female) report smelling cigar smoke. This was confirmed by other participants on the same tours. Bedford Springs is a no smoking resort, and no one was seen smoking in the vicinity.

While walking the corridors of the "Evitt Building" on the 1st floor during the tour, the door of one of the rooms we previously identified as 'haunted" (as reported by guests and staff) suddenly began to move back and forth, as if the door was stuck and couldn't be opened. This was visually witnessed (and heard) by four individuals on the tour. The room was unoccupied at the time.

Note:

Directly in front of the room, on the opposite wall, is a photograph of former guests of the hotel. The photograph was taken in the 1890's. In that photograph, along with a number of guests of both sexes, is the man whose photographs hangs in the "Crystal Dining Room", and the one who may have been photographed recently in the indoor pool area. Coincidence?

At the top of the stairs, next to the "Colonnade Ballroom", there is a hat display. One of the hats, a blue one, has been seen worn by a woman in Victorian dress who walks down the hall, through the door, then turns right to the present day "First Ladies Lounge" (the previous "Garden Room") and then disappears. The 'ghostly presence' has been seen by at least three different individuals at different times. These individuals did NOT check to see if the hat in the display was missing.

While talking about this perceived presence, in front of the hat display, one of the guests on the tour took a photo of all of us. The photo shows an anomalous large, and solid, 'mist' in the center of the photo. Various photographs were subsequently taken to re-create the event, including putting a finger in front of the lens. The same (or similar) image was not re-produced.

Post-Tour Experiences

A number of uncanny experiences occurred to guests after they attended the ghost tour. Many of these were associated with individuals who identified the name of "Anna" as the little girl who haunts the indoor pool area. One of those individuals was an elderly woman, who was accompanied by her grandchildren on the tour. In an email, she reported noises in her room at night.

She had placed a few hard candies (still in their wrappers) on the dresser in her room. These hard candies, as an after dinner treat, are available for guests as they leave the restaurant area of the hotel. Awakened by the noise, she thought they possibly came from a small mouse in the room. She did not investigate. When she awoke the next morning, she found them unwrapped, and the candies missing. Did a little girl take them, or was it just a mouse?

Another guest on the tour also had an uncanny experience in his room after the tour. While watching TV with his girlfriend, they saw a suitcase move and fall off the bed. At the time, they were resting peacefully on the bed. He too had identified the little girl as "Anna" in the solarium.

These are just two of the experiences that have occurred to recent guests on the tour. There are others. As we continue to do the tour, and tell the ghost stories that are associated with particular Bedford Springs spaces (and perhaps specific memories of past (and still attached) guests), we will continue to document these uncanny presences of the past in the present at Bedford Springs.

<u>Summary</u>

Bedford Springs is a 'storied' landscape, a well-worn book of emotion, time, space, and memory. This provides the guest, no matter how ephemeral the visit, with unique experiences that continue to mean something. This 'something' is not something 'paranormal', a 'ghost hunting' experience. It is a social encounter, and a relationship to place, that has provided meaning for more than a few guests, some of which continue years, even decades, after their 'final' stay there.

Part of the process in which this meaning is created involves the way in which contemporary guests experience the past in the present. These become stories of encounters, a mode of socialization in which presence is more than simply taking photographs that will adorn a home, or documents that remain enclosed in cupboards or desks.

These are experiences that locate Bedford Springs in time, within a particular memory, and of a specific space that more precisely (and emotionally) locate one's (and those of others) presence there. Bedford Springs is a homage, both to its past and those of the past of others who have visited (again and again) there. As a sensual medium, 'ghostly presence' there is another way of telling the "Bedford Springs Experience" without the need for words in a written narrative.

This experience is portioned in terms of time and memory, not architecture and renovation. Within these layers are tracks of presence one can follow across space, ones not burdened by walls, doors, changes in spatial functions, or the addition of new furnishings/decor, even indifference or skepticism. The presence of 'ghosts' serve as orientation points of remembrance of situations, events, and activities that still matter.

Haunting spaces are entwined there as 'knots' of meaningful associations that are not so different from the historical photographs and documents that are displayed there. This humanizes the place, not makes it spooky. It actively creates an enduring place out of space, as memories continue to accumulate, further enriching the social ambiance.

These memories maintain the social bond where people met and became "best friends forever". This is a Bedford Springs endorsement for something more than economic value. It created a different form of 'wealth': a sociability that endures from the past to this day. This is Bedford Springs' "buried treasure", the 'ghost stories' that lay hidden (and until recently) largely remained unspoken, ignored, and relegated to the dark recesses of 'fringe' thought and understanding.

The geographer, Yi-Fu Tuan (1974), has coined two terms that are significant for discussing this other type of "Bedford Springs Experience". These terms are "topophilia" and "topophobia". Topophilia refers to a love or affection for a place, a sense of belonging, a 'home' away from home. It is why guests return again and again to Bedford

Springs. They once 'haunted' the place, and some still do.

Topophobia is the reverse, a fear of place where one feels insecure. It is the reverse of people who 'haunt' because those with topophobia do NOT return. The 'ghostly presences at Bedford Springs reflect, by personal stories of attraction and attachment we tell on the tour, and reinforce the concept of topophilia, not one that is topophobic. Certainly, the 'ghosts' who remain attached there have that sense of belonging.

In contrast, most perceived haunted locations, especially those portrayed on TV programs, in movies, and on social media are part of a topophobic image. They are places that are intentionally meant to project fear and insecurity, certainly not a 'homely' feeling.

The hauntings at Bedford Springs illustrate the manner in which place memories and experiences are deeply embedded to certain spaces as a form of nostalgia. It also shows that these hauntings occur in places in which past and present coalesce and entangle in a positive (rather than negative) way. This finds a new and different unity of expression for 'ghostly presence'. It also follows closely the original meaning of 'haunt': to frequent a place, rather than 'terrorize' it.

Those former guests who return (again and again) played an active role in recalling the 'Bedford Springs Experience' in a profound, positive sense. The 'return' of some of them as 'ghostly presences' link persons, situations, acts, and events, placing the haunting into a landscape of remembrance. This is no 'ordinary' landscape. The presence of 'ghosts' there prevents the 'ordinary' sense of an affecting contestation, one negatively-charged, to surface there. Stability takes precedence over conflict and confrontation.

Such an overt, mostly harmonious, surface usually is a sign that a location is socially dead, lacks meaning, and is irrelevant. But Bedford Springs is different. Certainly its history is not one completely harmonious. But based on our research, and what occurs during (and after) the ghost tours, these uncanny materializations are more related to cultural resonance in harmony with the past, not a 'break' in attitude, behavior, or a place where "best friends forever" can't endure. The 'ghostly presences' also do not conflict with the presence of the past that is exhibited there in historical displays and photographs.

The 'ghostly' narrative that is spoken on the tour speaks of endless diversity, flows of context-specific meaning and significance in situated acts that have created a unique, non-paranormal sense of experience through time. The materializations of past presence continue to 'haunt' contemporary reality in a positive (some may even call 'entertaining') way.

As an archaeologist, I always 'dig deeper' to find out what is really going on in these perceived hauntings. Taking a phenomenological perspective this digging deep does not necessarily mean a vertical movement downward, representing a 'break' between past and present.

These 'ghostly presences' reside on the surface, manifesting all around us.

But this sense of the presence of the past requires acceptance and recognition on the part of the present. That is what we try to impart to the contemporary guests on the tour. It begins with active participation by them, and the possible future observation (not expectation) of what might occur. This participant-observer approach is a hallmark of traditional anthropological fieldwork.

On the tour, our narrative involves a description of the ghost stories associated with particular spaces, even though that space may have changed function and appearance through time. Our descriptions and their observations become entangled social acts. This allows the guests to become the contemporary counterparts of a continuing story that still 'haunts' because it has yet to end.

At Bedford Springs, the past and present continue into the future. That is the 'Bedford Springs Experience'......

<u>Photo 28:</u> An archive of records in the basement of the Anderson House (museum).

<u>Bibliography</u>

Bell, Michael Mayerfeld. 1997. The Ghosts of Place. *Theory and Society* 26(6): 813-836.

Benediktson, Karl and Lund, Karin Anna. 2013. Introduction: Starting a Conversation with Landscape in *Conversation with Landscape.* Edited by Karl Benediktson. Ashgate: University of Iceland.

Condren, Conal. 1985. *The Status and Appraisal of Classic Texts: An Essay on Political Theory, its Inheritance, and the History of Ideas.* Princeton: Princeton University Press.

Crocker, William. 1993. Canela Relationships with Ghosts: This-Worldly or Otherworldly Empowerment. *Latin American Anthropological Review* 5(2): 71-78.

Dawdy, Sharon Lee. 2016. *Patina: A Profane Archaeology.* Chicago: University of Chicago Press.

Deetz, James. 1998. Discussion: Archaeologists as Storytellers. *Historical Archaeology* 32(1): 94-96.

Gibson, J. 1986 (1979). *The Ecological Approach to Visual Perception.* Hillsdale, New Jersey: Lawrence Erlbaum.

Holloway, J. 2010. Legend-Tripping in Spooky Places: Ghost Tourism and Infrastructures of Enchantment. *Environment and Planning D.* 28: 618-637.

Illouz, Eva. 2007. *Cold Intimacies: The Making of Emotional Capitalism.* Cambridge: Polity.

Krueger, J. and T. Szanto. 2016. Extended Emotions. *Philosophy Compass* 11:863-878.

MacCannell, D. 1973. Staged Authenticity: Arrangements of Social Space in Tourist Settings. *American Journal of Sociology* 79: 589-603.

Melotti, Maxiano. 2016. Gladiator for a Day: Tourism, Archaeology, and Themed Parks in Rome in *Time and Temporality in Theme Parks.* F. Carla, F. Freitag, S. Mittermeier, and A. Schwarz (Editors). Hanover: Webrhahn. pp. 131-153.

Mink, Louis. 1987. Narrative Form as a Cognitive Instrument in *Historical Understanding.* Edited by B. Fay, E. Golob, and R. Vann. Ithaca: Cornell University Press. pp. 182-203.

Muecke, Stephen. 2006. Contingency and Ritual on the Islands of Ghosts: New Ethnography in Madagascar? In *Technologies of Magic: A Cultural Study of Ghosts, Machines, and the Uncanny.* Edited by John Potts and Edward Scheer. University of Sydney, Australia: Power Publications. pp. 92-111.

Nora, P. 1989. Between Memory and History. *Representations* 26: 7-24.

Potts, John. 2006. The Idea of the Ghost in *Technologies of Magic: A Cultural Study of*

Ghosts, Machines, and the Uncanny. Edited by John Potts and Edward Scheer. University of Sydney, Australia: Power Publications. pp. 78-91.

Sabol, John G. 2016. *The Haunting of the Omni Bedford Springs Resort.* Bedford, Pennsylvania: Ghost Excavation Books, Inc.

Schwartz, R. 1985. The Power of Pictures. *The Journal of Philosophy.* 82(12): 711-720.

Seamon, David. 1980. Body-Subject, Time-Space Routines, and Place-Ballets in *The Human Experience of Space and Place.* Edited by Anne Buttimer and David Seamon. London: Croom Held, Ltd. pp. 148-165.

Shanks, Michael and Connie Svabo. 2013. Archaeology and Photography: A Pragmatology in *Reclaiming Archaeology: Beyond the Tropes of Modernity.* Edited by Alfonzo Gonzalez-Ruibal. London: Routledge. pp. 89-102.

Smith, Benjamin and Richard Vokes. 2008. Introduction: Haunting Images. *Visual Anthropology. 21: 283-291.*

Sontag, Susan. 1977. *On Photography.* New York: Picador.

Thomas, Julian. 1993. The Hermeneutics of Megalithic Space in C. Tilley (Editor) *Interpretative Archaeology.* Oxford: Berg. pp. 73-97.

Thrift, Nigel. 2008. *Non-Representational Theory: Space, Politics, Affect.* London: Routledge.

Tilley, C. 2004. *The Materiality of Stone: Explorations in Landscape Phenomenology.* London: Berg.

Wilson, Patty. 2013. *Haunted Western Pennsylvania: Ghosts and Strange Phenomena of Pittsburgh, Erie, and the Laurel Highlands.* Mechanicsburg, Pennsylvania: Stackpole Books.

Witmore, C. 2009. Prolegomena to Open Pasts: On Archaeological Memory Practices. *Archaeologies* 5(3): 511-545.

Yi-Fu, Tuan. 1974. *Topophilia: A Study of Environmental Perception, Attitudes, and Values.* Englewood Cliffs, New Jersey: Prentice-Hall, Inc.

About the Author

John Sabol is an archaeologist, cultural anthropologist, actor, and author. As an archaeologist, he has unearthed past material remains in excavations and site surveys in England, Mexico, and at various sites in the United States (including Eastern South Dakota, the Tennessee River Valleys, and in Pennsylvania). His anthropological fieldwork includes the studies of "spirits" in the religious beliefs of the afterlife among various cultural groups in Mexico (Mixtec, Zapotec, Lacandon, Nahuatl, and Otomi). His acting career includes "ghosting" performances of various characters and scenarios in more than 35 movies, TV shows, and documentaries. He has appeared in the A&E TV series, Paranormal State as an investigative consultant.

He has written over thirty books. These include: *Ghost Excavator (2007), Ghost Culture (2007), Gettysburg Unearthed (2007), Battlefield Hauntscape (2008), The Anthracite Coal Region:*

The Archaeology of its Haunting Presence (2008), The Politics of Presence: Haunting Performances on the Gettysburg Battlefield (2008), Bodies of Substance, Fragments of Memories: An Archaeological Sensitivity to Ghostly Presence (2009), Phantom Gettysburg (2009), Digging Deep: An Archaeologist Unearths a Haunted Life (2009), The Re-Hauntings of Gettysburg (2010), Digging Up Ghosts (2011), The Haunted Theatre (2011), Haunting Archaeologies (2012), Beyond the Paranormal: Unearthing An Extended "Normal" at Haunted Locations (2013), Burnside Bridge Hauntscape: The Excavation of a Civil War Soundscape (2013), The Gettysburg Battlefield Experience (2013), The Good Death and The Civil War (2014), Centralia: A Vision of Ruin (2014), Altered States: Making the Extraordinary Ordinary Again (2014), Archaeology and Ghosts: A Relational Entanglement (2014), Anthracite Heritage: A Still Unmined Landscape (2014), Performances in Haunted Space: An Afterlife in Ruin (2014), Haunting Presences, Ruins, and Ghostly

Entanglements (2015), An Archaeology Without Borders: Performance Excavations in Embedded/Entangled Fields (2016).

His recent speaking engagements include the T.A.G. (Theoretical Archaeology Group) Conference at the University of California, Berkeley, at the Space and Place Conference in Prague, Czech Republic, the TAG Conference at the University in Buffalo, New York, Exploring the Extraordinary Conference in York, England, the C.H.A.T. archaeological conference also in York, and the GHost Conference at the University of London, London, England.

His investigative reports have been published in such diverse venues as Haunted Times Magazine, Tennessee Anthropologist, and the online journal, ParaAnthropology. He has been a frequent guest on numerous radio and internet talk shows, among them, Beyond the Edge Radio, The Paranormal View, Para X Radio, Blog Talk Radio, The Grand Dark Conspiracy, and Rusty O'Nhiall's

"Mysterious and Unexplained" on PsiFM (Australia). He was a university professor in Mexico for 11 years, teaching both undergraduate and graduate courses on the anthropology of tourism. He has also been featured on public educational TV for U.S. and foreign markets, and has worked on international educational documentaries (in Spain).

He has a M.A. in Anthropology/Archaeology (University of Tennessee), and a B.A. in Sociology/Anthropology (Bloomsburg University). He has also attended Penn State University, the University of Pittsburgh, the University of the Americas (Cholula, Puebla, Mexico), and has studied theatre and method acting in Mexico City.

He can be reached via email at cuicospirit@hotmail.com. His website is: **www.ghostexcavation.com** and he can be found on Facebook ("Ghost Excavations with John Sabol").

Photo 29: Unlocking the secrets of the past in the basement/museum

To be continued....